Dirty Jobs
Oil Rig Operator

Steve Goldsworthy

MEDIA ENHANCED BOOKS
AV²
BY WEIGL™
ADDED VALUE • AUDIO VISUAL

www.av2books.com

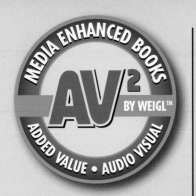

MEDIA ENHANCED BOOKS
AV²
BY WEIGL™
ADDED VALUE • AUDIO VISUAL

AV² provides enriched content that supplements and complements this boo[k]
Weigl's AV² books strive to create inspired learning and engage young min[ds]
in a total learning experience.

Your AV² Media Enhanced books come alive with...

Audio
Listen to sections of
the book read aloud.

Key Words
Study vocabulary, and
complete a matching
word activity.

Video
Watch informative
video clips.

Quizzes
Test your knowledge.

Embedded Weblinks
Gain additional information
for research.

Slide Show
View images and
captions, and prepare
a presentation.

Try This!
Complete activities and
hands-on experiments.

... and much, much more[!]

Go to **www.av2books.com**,
and enter this book's
unique code.

BOOK CODE

Y479361

AV² by Weigl brings you media
enhanced books that support
active learning.

Published by AV² by Weigl
350 5th Avenue, 59th Floor
New York, NY 10118
Websites: www.av2books.com   www.weigl.com

Library of Congress Control Number: 2014934861

ISBN 978-1-4896-1002-7 (hardcover)
ISBN 978-1-4896-1003-4 (softcover)
ISBN 978-1-4896-1004-1 (single user e-book)
ISBN 978-1-4896-1005-8 (multi user e-book)

Printed in the United States of America in North Mankato, Minnesota

1 2 3 4 5 6 7 8 9 0   18 17 16 15 14

032014
WEP150314

Project Coordinator: Aaron Carr
Designer: Mandy Christiansen

Every reasonable effort has been made to trace ownership and to obtain
permission to reprint copyright material. The publishers would be
pleased to have any errors or omissions brought to their attention so that
they may be corrected in subsequent printings.

Weigl acknowledges Getty Images as its primary image supplier for
this title.

Contents

What Is an Oil Rig Operator?

Oil rig operators are men and women who work on oil rigs. Oil rigs drill for **crude oil**. Operators work as a team to operate the drills and pumps on a rig. Crude oil production is a very important industry that provides raw materials for other industries such as **manufacturing**.

Oil rig operators build a large, towering structure called a derrick. The derrick sits on top of a platform. The platform supports all of the operators, machinery, and equipment used on the oil rig. These platforms may be positioned over land or over water. Ships or barges are often used as the supporting platforms for offshore oil rigs.

Many Names, One Job

Rotary Drill Operators, called "Drillers," are the team leaders on the **rig platform**. They operate the rotary equipment and mud pumps. Derrickhands carefully guide tools such as tubing in and out of the well that contains the **drill string**. Leasehands, sometimes called "roustabouts," assist the operator and the derrickhands. They clean, repair, and maintain the equipment. They also inspect the flow line that pumps mud into the hole.

The United States contains only **1.6** percent of the world's oil reserves.

On August 27, 1859, operators in Titusville, Pennsylvania, drilled the first oil well.

Americans used more than 367 million gallons (1.3 billion liters) of gasoline per day in 2011. That's enough gasoline to fill 556 Olympic-sized swimming pools.

Oil rig operators know their work gives people the resources they need to live their lives.

Where They Work

Oil rig workers work either on land-based or offshore oil rigs. Most land-based oil rigs are far away from places like shopping malls and restaurants. Workers often stay in hotels. If the rig is in a remote area such as a forest or prairie, the company sets up a camp. A camp has everything workers might need, including living quarters and entertainment.

Offshore oil rigs are like small floating cities. Workers have their own private rooms. These rigs also have recreation facilities, gyms, saunas, and 24-hour cafeterias.

Offshore oil rigs are often located in remote areas. The oil rigs must be equipped with everything the operators need.

Around the Clock Work

An oil rig operates 24 hours a day, seven days a week. Oil rig operators work long, hard hours far away from family and friends. Each shift is usually 12 hours long. This is much longer than the usual 8-hour work shift.

Workers on offshore oil rigs are brought to the rig by helicopter.

A Dirty Job

Working on an oil rig is a dirty job. Oil rig operators must work with dirt, mud, and crude oil. Workers take **mud samples** throughout their shift. The mud and grime often splashes and covers their clothing and hair.

Oil Drilling Dangers

Working on an oil rig is thought to be one of the most dangerous jobs in the world. It is hard work that takes strength and concentration. Drilling for crude oil can cause rock layers to collapse. Offshore oil rigs can become unstable if this happens. Workers are often around highly flammable chemicals. There is always a danger of fire.

Explosions and fires are major dangers on an oil rig. In 2008, 4,340 workers in the U.S. died while working on oil rigs.

At sea, the weather can change suddenly. Many oil rigs in the Gulf of Mexico are at risk from hurricanes. Workers must leave the rig if a storm heads their way.

Platforms are equipped with airtight escape pods for emergencies. Workers can climb into these small vessels and lower themselves into the ocean to escape danger.

In 2005, Hurricane Katrina destroyed 30 oil rig platforms in the Gulf of Mexico.

Safety is a serious issue on oil rigs. Operators must take many precautions to keep themselves safe while working.

Gasoline Production

Gasoline production begins with a process called fractional **distillation**. Trucks or pipelines take crude oil to a refinery. A furnace heats the oil to 600° Fahrenheit (316° Celsius). The hot vapors rise into a tall **fractioning** tower. As the liquid cools, it separates into several parts. Heavier parts such as waxes and **lubricants** settle on trays at the bottom. Lighter parts like gasoline collect at the top. Workers remove the gasoline and further refine it with more chemicals.

19.4 gallons (73.4 L) of gasoline can be created from a 42-gallon (159 L) barrel of oil.

One American uses an average of

3.5
gallons

(13.25 L) of oil a day.

72 percent of crude oil becomes fuel, including gasoline, jet fuel, and diesel.

There are about
1.3 trillion barrels
of oil left in the world.

All in a Day's Work

On land-based oil rigs, workers will often travel to the rig in their own vehicles. Sometimes, they go together in crew trucks. Offshore workers live and work on the rig.

Workers on offshore rigs begin in the cafeteria with breakfast. They must eat well to keep their strength up for the long day ahead. Some workers will climb the derrick tower to guide various pipes into position. Others work down below, on the deck, with the mud pump. They will often work 14 days straight. Then, they will have a break of one to three weeks. Many workers return home to visit families and friends during their breaks.

Oil rig work is often seasonal in some areas. In colder regions, winter is the best time to drill.

It takes about 300 people to keep an oil rig running 24 hours a day.

The British Petroleum deep water platform Holstein is 990 feet (301.7 meters) tall from the bottom of the sea bed to the top of its oil derrick. That is taller than the Eiffel Tower.

Oil rigs can cost $650,000 a day to operate.

From the Rig to Your Car

Extracting crude oil from the ground or seabed is just the beginning of the fuel-making process. Crude oil undergoes many other steps, including refining and processing, before it can be used as fuel. Other substances, known as petroleum by-products, come from crude oil. Things like glue and cosmetics are made from these by-products.

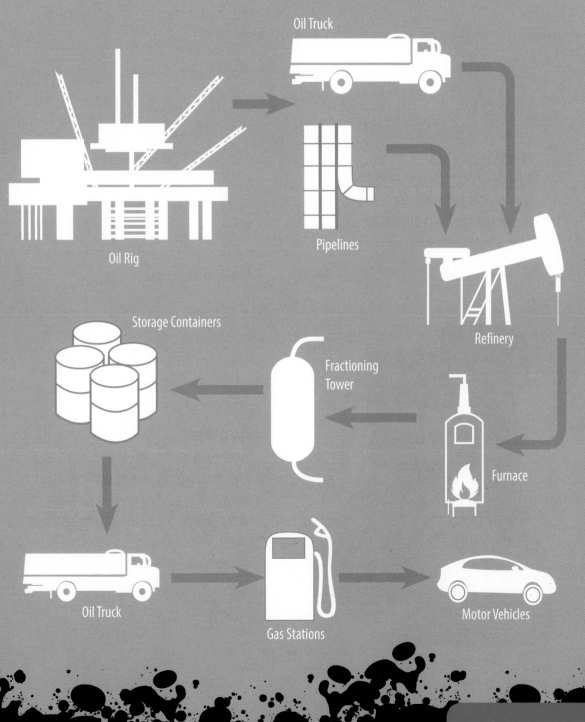

Oil Truck

Pipelines

Oil Rig

Refinery

Storage Containers

Fractioning Tower

Furnace

Oil Truck

Gas Stations

Motor Vehicles

Staying Safe

Besides dangers from machinery and weather, there are many other dangers to workers on an oil rig. Many operators work at great heights. They must be strapped to safety ropes to keep from falling. Noisy machinery can damage hearing. Operators must take frequent breaks during their long work shifts so they do not get tired and make mistakes.

Hard Hat

A hard hat protects operators from falling tools and material. A strong plastic shell deflects objects. Inside, foam and straps absorb impacts.

Boots

Steel-toed boots protect a worker's feet from falling tools and equipment. Steel soles on the bottom prevent nails and other sharp objects from piercing workers' feet.

Safety First

Many oil rig operators buy their own safety equipment. Some oil rig companies provide certain pieces of equipment to their employees.

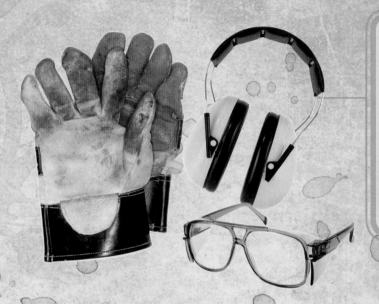

Gloves, Masks, and Earphones

Gloves protect a worker's hands from various harmful chemicals used to lubricate pipes. Earplugs and other types of ear protection protect a worker's hearing from damage. Plastic safety glasses protect eyes from mud and debris.

Coveralls

Like gloves, coveralls protect a worker from the various lubricants and chemicals used in the drilling process.

Tools of the Trade

Oil rig operators must know how to operate a number of heavy machines. A common tool on an oil rig is the **hydraulic tongs**. These tongs turn and lift the rig's drill string. They hang from an arm near the rotary table. It usually takes two or three people to move the tongs. Operators clamp the device around the pipe going down to the drill bit.

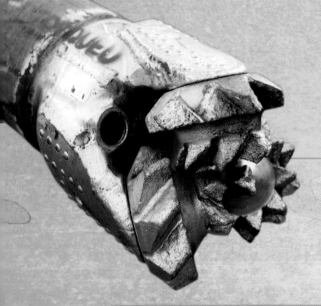

Drill Bit

The drill bit connects to the end of the drill string. The whole bit rotates while it grinds and cuts rock. It also allows for the flow of debris up through the hole.

Mud Pump

The mud pump is a high-pressure pump used to circulate drilling fluid, called mud. It runs by an engine or motor. It pumps mud into and out of the hole.

Rotary Table

The rotary table is the spinning section of the platform. It turns the drill string in a clockwise direction. It also supports the series of steel pipes called the drilling assembly. Several workers must work together to move the device into place.

Workers built the first offshore oil rig in the Gulf of Mexico in 1938. The rig had a wooden platform and stood on pine **pilings.** The machines were very simple. Operators used their hands to do most of the work. Early technology involved a steam-powered cable tool. A large chisel on the end cut through the rock.

Now

An oil rig is a very complex job site. Operators use highly advanced machines for drilling. Dozens of people in the rig's control room use computers to monitor the flow of oil.

The Oil Rig Operator's Role

Oil rig operators play an important role in producing crude oil. They provide the physical labor needed to keep the drills digging. After workers establish a **drill line**, a service rig replaces the drilling rig. Operators continue to work on the service rigs. They monitor the pumping of crude oil from the underground **reservoir**.

"It's a dirty job, but someone has to do it."

Oil Refining

Refining crude oil is the only way to make the oil useful. Refining is a chemical process that separates the oil and removes impurities. The separate parts created by refining include kerosene for flame lanterns and **asphalt** for making roads.

Oil rig operators are dedicated workers who do not mind working miles from home.

Things Made from Oil...

Many items used every day are made from oil, such as

plastic hangers, egg cartons, and glue.

It takes 8 gallons (30 L) of oil to make one car tire.

Asphalt has been used to make **11 million miles** (17.7 million kilometers) of road in the world.

Almost 5 percent of all oil products go into making plastic.

Becoming an Oil Rig Operator

Operating an oil rig is a physically demanding job. Being strong and fit is important, because operators must work with heavy machinery for long shifts. A high school diploma is required. Most training happens on the job. Trade schools and technical colleges offer courses in oil field work. Operators might have certificates in heavy equipment operation, basic mechanics, and welding.

Salaries for oil rig operators vary depending on the demands of the position. Oil rig operators are paid well for their work. Operators with more experience and education make a higher salary. Beginners with less than a year of experience can expect to earn $45,000 a year.

Average Salary per Year

Steward	$45,000
Leasehand	$55,000
Painters	$58,000
Rig welders, radio operators	$60,000
Storemen	$60,000
Medics	$70,000
Mud engineers	$110,000
Subsea engineers	$135,000
Rig foreman	$200,000

If you do not mind getting dirty, becoming an oil rig operator could be the career for you.

Is This Career for You?

A career as an oil rig operator can be tough. It means being away from family and friends for weeks or months at a time. The shifts are long and hard. Operators who are skilled and work well in groups can work their way up quickly. They may become managers within a few years.

✓ Training

Workers must have the proper training before stepping onto a rig. Many oil companies require workers to have Offshore Survival & Fire fighting certification. They must also have first-aid training and various safety certificates.

✓ Education

Besides a high school diploma, workers must have a driver's license so they can drive to and from their work site.

✓ Application

Job openings are often posted on the Internet. Oil companies and drilling companies also post entry-level jobs on their websites. Check a company's human resources page for job listings. You can also look for local jobs at operations in your area.

Career Connections

Plan your oil rig operator career with this activity. Follow the instructions outlined in the steps to complete the process of becoming an oil rig operator.

 1. Speak to local oil rig operators. They can answer your questions and give you an inside look into the position.

 **4.** Call or write to oil companies. Say that you are interested in an oil rig operating position and ask for advice on how to apply.

 **2.** Visit a job fair or a university career center to find out more information about working in the oil rig industry.

3. Work on your resumé. A good resumé that shows your strongest skills can go a long way toward attracting the attention of potential employers.

1. Decide if you have the personality and attitude to be an oil rig operator. If you do not mind a dirty job, can work flexible hours, and are in good physical shape, this may be the job for you.

2. Consider the skills you will need to have. Having a valid driver's license or a certificate to operate heavy machinery will be a bonus.

3. Contact employers for requirements. Look at oil and drilling companies. Get in touch with them and find out what they are looking for from potential applicants.

4. Apply for the position and arrange an interview. If successful, come to the interview with knowledge of the industry and your skills.

Quiz

1. What is another name for leasehands?

2. When was the first oil well drilled?

3. What is another name for the fluid used in drilling?

4. During oil refinement, what temperature is crude oil heated to?

5. When is it estimated that oil reserves will run out?

6. How many days does an oil rig operator typically work on a rig?

7. What is the machine that turns the drill string and drill bit?

8. When was the first offshore oil rig built in the Gulf of Mexico?

9. How many gallons (liters) of oil does it take to make a car tire?

10. What is the average yearly salary of a leasehand?

Answers:
1. Roustabouts
2. August 27, 1859, in Titusville, Pennsylvania
3. Mud
4. 600°F (316°C)
5. By the year 2053
6. 14 days
7. The rotary table
8. 1938
9. 8 gallons (30 L)
10. $55,000

Key Words

asphalt: a thick black substance mixed with sand to make roads

crude oil: raw oil that has not yet been refined into a usable form

distillation: the process of purifying liquid by heating and cooling

drill line: a twisted wire rope used to help lift and lower the drill string

drill string: a series of connected pipes that spins in the hole of the drilling site

fractioning: to break into smaller pieces

hydraulic tongs: a tool or machine, joined at one end like a crab's claw, used to grip and pick up something

lubricants: substances such as grease or mud used to make something move smoothly

manufacturing: an industry in which products are produced from raw materials by hand or by the use of machinery

mud samples: small selections of mud collected from the oil rig for research purposes

pilings: columns of wood or steel that are driven into the ground, like legs of a structure

reservoir: a large body of liquid, like an underground lake

rig platform: the main deck of an on-land or offshore oil rig

rotary: something that revolves around a center, like a spinning pipe

Index

Log on to www.av2books.com

AV² by Weigl brings you media enhanced books that support active learning. Go to www.av2books.com, and enter the special code found on page 2 of this book. You will gain access to enriched and enhanced content that supplements and complements this book. Content includes video, audio, weblinks, quizzes, a slide show, and activities.

AV² Online Navigation

Audio
Listen to sections of the book read aloud

Book Pages
AV² pages directly correspond to pages in the book.

Video
Watch informative video clips.

Key Words
Study vocabulary, and complete a matching word activity.

Embedded Weblinks
Gain additional information for research.

Quizzes
Test your knowledge.

Slide Show
View images and captions, and prepare a presentation.

Try This!
Complete activities and hands-on experiments.

AV² was built to bridge the gap between print and digital. We encourage you to tell us what you like and what you want to see in the future.

Sign up to be an AV² Ambassador at www.av2books.com/ambassador.

Due to the dynamic nature of the Internet, some of the URLs and activities provided as part of AV² by Weigl may have changed or ceased to exist. AV² by Weigl accepts no responsibility for any such changes. All media enhanced books are regularly monitored to update addresses and sites in a timely manner. Contact AV² by Weigl at 1-866-649-3445 or av2books@weigl.com with any questions, comments, or feedback.